The Virtues of the Holy Qur'an

The Light, Inc.
26 Worlds Fair Dr. Suite C
Somerset, New Jersey, 08873, USA
www.thelightpublishing.com

Title	The Virtues of the Holy Qur'an
Author	Ayhan Tekines
Editor	Jane Louise Kandur
Art Director	Engin Ciftci
Published by	The Light, Inc.
Printed by	Caglayan A.S. - Izmir, 2006
ISBN	1-932099-29-8

Printed in Turkey

CONTENTS

1- WHAT IS THE QUR'AN?...............5

2- THE VIRTUES OF THE QUR'AN 8

3- THE QUR'AN AND RAMADAN........10

4- THE QUR'AN AND OUR HOMES.......12

5- DEVOTION TO THE QUR'AN 14

6- THE VIRTUES OF QUR'AN
   LESSONS................................17

7- THE VIRTUES OF LEARNING
   THE QUR'AN 19

8- THE VIRTUES OF PARENTS'
   TEACHING THEIR CHILDREN HOW
   TO READ THE QUR'AN 23

9- THE VIRTUES OF READING
   THE QUR'AN 26

10- THE REWARDS FOR READING
    THE QUR'AN 31

WHAT IS THE QUR'AN?

"It is a treasure that makes one need nothing but itself."

The Qur'an is a message that explains Allah's spiritual treasures that are seen on earth and in the skies; it provides information about the unknown. It is the sun, the foundation, and plan of Islam, and it is an eternal translation of the universe. It is a generous, heavenly book that Allah has sent us in order to fulfill all our needs, whether these needs are physical or spiritual. Allah's most beautiful Names and His Throne are the source of the Qur'an. When we speak about "the Word of Allah" we mean the Qur'an. Through it the Creator of the earth and the skies speaks to us; it is an edict by the Maker of the universe, the word of Allah, the Lord of all beings.

The Qur'an is a book of divine laws, a book of wonderful messages that is comparable with the value and worth of human beings. The Qur'an came from Allah and was created within the world of human beings. It is a miraculous book that holds the essence of all knowledge; it is a book whose wonders are never exhausted. It includes religious judgments, precious knowledge, and it teaches us what to say when praying and how to pray. It is the mother of all books. The Prophet, peace be upon him, says of the Qur'an, "It is a treasure that makes one need nothing but itself" (Majma' al-Zawa'id, 7, 158). In this hadith the Prophet (pbuh) states that the Qur'an includes all kinds of knowledge, addresses all kinds of people, and offers solutions for all kinds of problems.

The Qur'an is the life source of souls, the basis of morality, and the essence of prayers. The Prophet (pbuh) says, "Be sure that the Qur'an is the feast offered by Allah" (Darimi, Fada'il al-Qur'an, 1). In this feast all kinds of food, savory and sweet, are on offer. Although each food might have a different taste and composition, everyone can find something they like in this feast. Saying, "One who comes to this feast will have no fear of hunger" 'Abd Allah ibn Mas'ud points to the fact that the Qur'an, with its rich content, holds solutions for everyone's troubles. Since it is the source of all the knowledge and information that Muslims take pride in, it has been said, "Islam is Qur'anic Civilization." The Prophet (pbuh) introduced and taught us this holy source. His words are the statements that best explain the contents of the Qur'an. In one of his hadiths, the Prophet (pbuh) says:

"(The Qur'an is such a book that) it includes news from past (nations which preceded you), the fitna (seditious events and internal conflicts, anarchy and subversion) to come after you until the time of Doomsday, and judgments, about the situations to take place among you. It is the only measure that divides truth from untruth. Everything in it is serious. Whoever abandons it fearing a tyrant and stops practicing (what the Qur'an says), will be ruined by Allah. Whoever looks for guidance anywhere else will be misguided by

Allah. Indeed, it is Allah's strongest rope (to hold on to). It is a remembrance full of wisdom, and a path that leads to the Truth. It saves those who observe it from misguidance (due to being seized by various temptations) and protects the tongues (speeches, communication) that recite it from ambiguity. Scholars can never satisfy their hunger for it. Its oft repetition does not weary the one who reads it, nor its pleasure decreases. Its fascinating aspects know no end. It is such a book that when the jinn heard it, they could not help saying: 'We have really heard a wonderful recital! It gives guidance to the right, and we have believed therein' (72:1-2). *One who speaks in its fashion speaks the truth. One who observes it will surely be rewarded. Whoever rules upon it judges justly. Whoever calls to it, calls to the Straight Path"* (Tirmidhi, Fada'il al-Qur'an, 14).

This hadith speaks of many characteristics of the Holy Qur'an. It is mentioned as being that which distinguishes truth from untruth, as being Allah's strongest guideline, as being the wise reminder, and the path to Allah. Distinguishing the truth from the untruth is one of the fundamental characteristics of the Qur'an. In this respect it is also called Furqan:

"Blessed is He Who sent down the Criterion upon His servant, so as to be a warner to all mankind" (25:1).

Stating that the Qur'an is universal, this verse emphasizes that the Furqan distinguishes the truth from the untruth, arranges the lives of those who assimilate Islam and shows what is good and what is bad. As stated in the above-mentioned hadith, the Qur'an is a strong guide sent by Allah to lead those who take hold of it to the true path. It consists of wise words and is a wise reminder. The Qur'an, with its infinite wisdom, states everything sufficiently for the needs of human beings. It provides believers with accurate reminders and advice while they are following the path that they should tread and living the lives that they should live. It is the most genuine path. It is a guide that prevents people from extremes, not only in subjects related to faith and prayers, but also in social, economic, and administrative matters.

THE VIRTUES OF THE QUR'AN

"It is a treasure that makes one need nothing but itself."

In order to be able to describe and understand the essence of the Qur'an you must be able to recognize its superior features. The Qur'an is the word of Allah, the Creator of all worlds and the Maker of all beings. It is the highest realization of Allah's most beautiful names. The Qur'an was not revealed for a single era or a particular nation. The richness of its content, the firmness of its judgments, and the gravity and harmony of its style show that the Qur'an is Allah's address to all humans. The value and importance of the Qur'an can better be understood in the following hadith: *"In the presence of Allah there is no word more precious than the Qur'an"* (Darimi, Fada'il al-Qur'an, 5).

In another hadith, *"The superiority of the word of Allah over other words is like Allah's superiority over His creations"* (Tirmidhi, Fada'il al-Qur'an, 25), the value of the Qur'an is emphasized.

Another superior characteristic of the Qur'an is the fact that it will intercede for people on the Day of Judgment. The Qur'an is such an intercessor that none of its demands will be refused. On the Day of Judgment it will protect those who read and observed it, it will intercede for them, and help them win eternal paradise. The Prophet (pbuh) encourages reading the Qur'an in the following hadith, *"Read the Qur'an! It will be such a wonderful intercessor on Doomsday."* The rest of the hadith tells us how the Qur'an will intercede: *"On Doomsday the Qur'an will speak (for those who read it) 'Lord, adorn him with honor.'*

That person will be adorned with honor. It will say, 'Lord, dress him in honor.' The person will be dressed in honor. He will be crowned with the crown of honor" (Tirmidhi, Fada'il al-Qur'an, 18).

The Qur'an is the word of Allah. Even a single letter from the Qur'an is more precious than everything else in the world. The value of the Qur'an should not be diminished by using it for mundane ends. It is dangerous to read the Qur'an to gain worldly rewards, and still more dangerous to claim to recite the Qur'an, yet then indoctrinate people in one's own opinions and ideas. The Prophet (pbuh) informs us that such people will appear in the future: *"Whoever reads the Qur'an should ask for his due from Allah. Someday people who read the Qur'an will appear, they will make the Qur'an a tool for their worldly desires"* (Tirmidhi, Fada'il al-Qur'an, 19). In this hadith the Prophet (pbuh) objects to asking for money in return for reading the Qur'an and for abusing it to gain worldly benefits.

THE QUR'AN AND RAMADAN

The holy month of Ramadan is the month of the Qur'an as much as it is the month of fasting.

The Qur'an is so precious and important that it increases the value of anything it is associated with. It has increased the value of time and space, honored the paper it is written on and the ink it is written with; it has made those who read and listen to it virtuous. The

Night of Qadr and the month of Ramadan, the month during which the Qur'an was revealed, get their value from the Qur'an. Ramadan is undoubtedly the most precious time in respect of the Qur'an. Ramadan and the reading of the Qur'an are intertwined. The reason for the increase in the amount of prayers during Ramadan is in order to read the Qur'an. The holy month of Ramadan is the month of the Qur'an as much as it is the month of fasting. The revelations started and ended in the month of Ramadan. Going into retreat to pray during the last ten days of Ramadan, the Prophet (pbuh) would chant all of the Qur'an in unison with the Archangel Gabriel during the month of Ramadan. Abu Hurayra tells of the Prophet's retreating and reading the Qur'an as follows:

"Gabriel used to repeat the recitation of the Qur'an with the Prophet (pbuh) once a year; he repeated it twice the year the Prophet (pbuh) died. The Prophet (pbuh) used to pray in retreat ten days a year; the year he died he prayed twenty days in retreat" (Bukhari, Fada'il al-Qur'an, 7).

Reading the Qur'an softens the hearts of those who read it and increases their mercy to other people. This is also the result of the charitable actions of giving to the poor during Ramadan. When the Prophet (pbuh) was reciting the Qur'an with Gabriel, the Prophet (pbuh) was very generous and would give anything that he was asked for. Ibn Abbas describes his state as follows:

"The Prophet (pbuh) was the most generous of all human beings. He would be more generous when he met Gabriel in Ramadan. Gabriel would meet him every night during Ramadan and teach him the Qur'an. The Prophet (pbuh) was more generous than a blessed wind in matters of good deed" (Bukhari, Sawm, 7).

THE QUR'AN AND OUR HOMES

"Do not turn your homes into graves. The Devil cannot go into a house where Surat al-Baqara is read."

It is the people who live in a place that make it valuable. Our homes are valuable if the Qur'an is being read, taught, and its orders are being obeyed there. As it is the remembrance of Allah that makes our mosques sacred, so it is the reading of the Book of Allah that brings abundance to our homes.

In this respect our homes and our mosques are equal. The Qur'an says of such houses:

"In the houses Allah allowed to be raised and His name to be mentioned therein, He is glorified therein, mornings and evenings; By men who are not distracted, by trading or trafficking, from mentioning Allah's Name, performing the prayer and giving the prescribed alms. They fear a day whereon the hearts and eye-sights shall be turned around" (24:36-37).

Although there are scholars who interpret the "houses" in this verse as being mosques, there are also those who interpret the "houses" as being the homes of believers. It is probable that both are being referred to. As we have seen, it is what is done in a place that brings value to that place.

The Qur'an is bounty and benefit for our homes. Bounty is not limited to an increase in wealth. Besides material benefits, it is important for all people, especially for a family, to be spiritually happy. The reading of the Qur'an softens the heart; thus, an environment of mercy and compassion, which is greatly needed in a family, will be established. In this respect, if the Qur'an is read in a house we can say that there is happiness and blessings there. It is related in a hadith: *"The house when the Qur'an is read in it enlarges for those who dwell in it; angels are present there, devils are driven away and that house becomes auspicious"* (Darimi, Fada'il al-Qur'an, 1). The physical spaciousness of a house is not something all families can have. However, if we want spiritual space and blessings, then we can turn our houses into places where Allah is remembered and the Qur'an is read.

Homes in which the Qur'an is not read are silent and isolated like graves. Just as the dead do not have a chance to gain merit by reading the Qur'an, the path to acquiring merit is closed for people who live in houses where the Qur'an is not read. Moreover, not reading the Qur'an might lead to problems of spirit and conscience, and later maybe even to death. The Prophet (pbuh) encourages us to read the Qur'an in our homes, saying, *"Do not turn your homes into graves. The Devil cannot go into a house where Surat al-Baqara is read"* (Tirmidhi, Fada'il al-Qur'an, 2).

Even if a person reads the Qur'an at work or in the mosque, he or she must also read it at home, too. Reading the Qur'an at home has the advantage of setting a good example for family members and teaching children to love the Qur'an. The hadith also refers to the fact that the Devil will disturb people who live in houses where the Qur'an is not read. If we want to revive our houses and keep the Devil and all evil away, then we should brighten up our homes by reading the Qur'an. We should not turn our houses into ruins by watching films and listening to music that damages our souls, occupies our minds, destroys our hearts and abuses our love.

DEVOTION TO THE QUR'AN

"Learn the Book of Allah, and live by its principles."

The first obligation for anyone who is familiar with the Qur'an is to follow and obey its commands. The Qur'an is a universal book whose address is not limited to time or space. The secret and miracle of staying anew is to be found here. The Qur'an, by advising a balanced life and by adopting permanent and ideal principles, has become the fountainhead from which all Islamic civilizations have attained their riches. The rays of light it emits in all directions have illuminated the world. With its purity and clarity, the Qur'an surges like an icy spring inviting all people and societies to come and drink from its truth, justice, order, and peace. After stating that he was soon to die, the Prophet (pbuh) said, *"I am leaving among you two weighty things: one being the Book of Allah in which there is right guidance and light, so hold fast to the Book of Allah and adhere to it. The second is the members of my household; I remind you (of your duties) to the members of my family"* (Muslim, Fada'il al-Sahaba, 36-37). Leaving the Qur'an as a guide to humanity and recommending his family as their leader and imam, the

Prophet (pbuh) stated that his followers would never digress from the true path as long as they held these two in trust. In another hadith he recommended "the Qur'an and his sunna" for his followers and underlined the similarity of his sunna and the social role of his family. Two principles are needed in order for a society not to fail. The first of these is the Holy Book that will give a direction to their thoughts, the book that holds the principles that enables a unified society, and that is unanimously accepted by all spheres of society. The second is the Prophet's family, which sets an example for society with their behavior and the sunna of the Prophet (pbuh) that contains the principles in his life.

Life finds its true meaning with the Qur'an. Abundance in life is proportional to one's acceptance of the Holy Qur'an as a life principle. Those who obey its principles improve their lives in the world and are saved in the hereafter.

"Surely, this Qur'an guides to that which is most upright and announces to the believers who do good works the good news that they shall have a reward" (17:9). The fact that the first Muslims conquered lands at an unprecedented pace and that they established a magnificent civilization was realized thanks to the Qur'an. The Prophet (pbuh) says, *"Allah will exalt some societies with the Qur'an and abase others"* (Ibn Maja, Muqaddima, 16). As stated in the hadith, those who observed the Qur'anic principles during the golden era were exalted, while those who disregarded it were deprived of the light of civilization brought by the Qur'an. Other nations may rise with different principles but in this hadith the rise of the Muslims is connected with the Qur'an. This is as true today as it was yesterday.

The Prophet (pbuh) ordered people to hold fast to the Qur'an in the future when turmoil and dissent would arise. At the root of dissension is the disregard of certain accepted rules. If people were to agree upon a single book, it would be easy to settle their problems. Little conflicts will not lead to the disturbance of unity and cooperation; on the contrary, they would broaden social life. To unite under the protective shade of the Qur'an is the only way to avoid all evil. When Huzayfa asked the Prophet (pbuh) how he could avoid the evil that would come in the future, the Prophet (pbuh) said, *"Study the Book of Allah, and live by its principles"* (Nasa'i, Sunan al-Kubra, 5, 18), showing that this is the only way to overcome future evils. Knowledge must be practiced. Unapplied knowledge is useless knowledge. There is little difference between possessing and not possessing knowledge if that knowledge is useless. The Prophet (pbuh) said that in the future knowledge would disappear. When a companion asked, *"We read the Qur'an, and teach it to our children. They will teach it to their children. How will knowledge disappear?"* the Prophet (pbuh) said, *"Don't you see? Are the Jews and Christians practicing the Torah (Tawrat) and the Gospel (Injil) in spite of reading them?"* (Ibn Maja, Fitan, 26). Unless the Qur'an is practiced and observed, the knowledge of the Qur'an will become obsolete. In the hadiths we see the companions' endeavors and sincerity in teaching the Qur'an. They were well aware of the necessity of handing the Qur'an down to following generations in order to protect religious knowledge. Giving the Qur'an the dominant place in our lives and behaving accordingly is not an easy virtue to maintain. However, it would not be correct to distance yourself from the Qur'an because you think that you cannot practice it properly. One of the companions once said that he did not memorize the Sura al-Baqara because he could not practice it fully. The Prophet (pbuh) told him, *"Study and teach the Qur'an. The state of the person who learns, reads, and practices the Qur'an is like a box filled with musk whose fragrance spreads everywhere. The state of the person who has learned the Qur'an but does not read and practice it is a musk-filled box whose lid is tightly secured"* (Tirmidhi, Fada'il al-Qur'an, 2). This analogy shows us that it is not correct to neglect learning the Qur'an in fear of not being able to practice it properly.

THE VIRTUES OF QUR'AN LESSONS

"Remember Me then and I will remember you.
Give thanks to Me and do not be ungrateful."

I n order to be guided by the Qur'an, we should be able to perceive its message correctly and obtain good knowledge of its decrees. The knowledge of the Qur'an is acquired by lessons and discussions. There are various hadiths on the virtues of Qur'an lessons. Not only teaching the Qur'an but also discussing on related topics, as well as studying commentaries were praised in hadiths, one of which is, *"One who sets off with the intention to gain knowledge, Allah facilitates for him (to orient himself toward) the path to Heaven. When a group of people sit in a mosque, read Allah's Book and discuss, sakina (divine serenity) descends on them, mercy covers them and angels surround them"* (Tirmidhi, Qiraah, 3). This hadith does not mention individual reading but points out to the merits of group study and discussion. Reading the Qur'an, even as an individual activity, is a very special way of worshiping. However, when believers gather with a unified motive to read the Qur'an or to study any

Qur'anic teachings, it is felt as if the skies are closer to earth and angels greet this sacred effort.

Qur'an lessons are not peculiar to mosques. Lessons carried out in houses are also praised. If the Qur'an is recited and studied in a house, that very house acquires a completely different identity and becomes on a par with a mosque in respect of its blessings. A hadith describes this state as, "*Sakina descends on those friends of Allah who gather in the houses of Allah, who recite the Qur'an, and who discuss it; grace covers them, angels surround them, and Allah talks of them when the angels are present*" (Muslim, Dhikr, 37). In the last sentence of this hadith, we can see an explanation of the verse:

"*Remember Me then and I will remember you. Give thanks to Me and do not be ungrateful*" (2:152). Several other hadiths describe how grace and angels descended on the Prophet's (pbuh) companions who recited the Qur'an.

Disputes and ambiguous interpretations concerning the Qur'an should be avoided. Although there are ambiguous verses in the Qur'an, they were revealed to make clear the limitations of man's knowledge. The most fundamental feature of the Qur'an is that it was revealed in a clear and understandable language. Thus, one should not depict the Qur'an as a book that contains controversial issues. It is this feature of the Qur'an that distinguishes it from other holy books. Its judgments are clear and certain; its principles are lucid and unambiguous. The Qur'an itself discusses this:

"*Alif, Lam, Ra. These are the verses of the clear Book. We have revealed it as an Arabic Qur'an, that perchance you may understand*" (12:1-2).

Since its meaning is clear, becoming involved in disputes over some verses only involves one's ego and lower self. To call people to the Qur'an means to call them to communal unity and accord; it means to call them to the faith of oneness. It is not a call to egotistical thoughts or ambitions. Therefore, the words of the Prophet (pbuh), "*Recite (and study) the Qur'an as long as you can agree on its interpretation, but when you have any difference of opinion (as regards its interpretation and meaning) then you should stop reciting it (for the time being)*" (Fada'il al-Qur'an, 37), should be our standard and we should not use the Qur'an to support our personal views.

THE VIRTUES OF LEARNING THE QUR'AN

"The most virtuous among you is he who teaches and learns the Qur'an."

T he first step in understanding and discussing the Qur'an is to learn how to read it. Learning to read the Qur'an used to be the first stage toward learning all sciences. Children used to learn how to read by reading the Qur'an; those studying sciences used to enter their educational lives by memorizing verses from it. Education in the Qur'an was regarded as the door to knowledge and was therefore encouraged. The Prophet (pbuh) tells of the affection Allah feels toward those who read the Qur'an, *"Verily, Allah has friends among mankind."* They asked, *"O Allah's messenger, who are they?"* He replied, *"The possessors of the Qur'an; they are Allah's beloved ones and His close friends"* (Ibn Maja, Muqaddima, 16). Reading the Qur'an raises the position of a person in the sight of Allah. Addressing Allah in person by reading His Word is the ultimate prayer that can draw people closer to Him.

Islam encourages the acquisition of knowledge. The best knowledge is that that is required by knowing Allah and affectionately obeying Him. It is only possible by reading the word of Allah and by addressing Him for believers to know Allah and to attain an ever-growing love for Him. As long as there is nothing inside us that attests to the Truth, any newly acquired knowledge will not enhance our skills, but will instead deepen our ignorance. Memorizing and learning the meanings of suras that tell us about the basic principles of the Qur'an will enlighten our conscience; they will become the light of our hearts and minds. Thus, the destruction of our inner world will be prevented. The Prophet (pbuh) mentions this reality in an analogy: *"Anyone who has nothing of the Qur'an within him is like an empty and derelict house"* (Tirmidhi, Fada'il al-Qur'an, 18). In this hadith it is said that the state of a person who does not know the Qur'an is like an empty house, with no one living in it. Just as a derelict house is of no use to humans, and just as it deteriorates every day, a person who does not read the Qur'an can be of no help, either to themselves or others. As long as this ignorance persists, the inner emptiness will deepen and their troubles will continue.

Unlike other good deeds, the promised reward for reading the Qur'an is ten times every letter, not every sura or every word, but every letter. Compared to other prayers, reading the Qur'an is a prayer that gains the greatest rewards in the shortest time. The reward for reading the Qur'an is stated in the following: *"Learn the Qur'an. Ten sawabs (rewards) will be given for every letter read in the Qur'an"* (Tirmidhi, Fada'il al-Qur'an, 16). Moreover, it has been said in some hadiths that the reading of some suras have greater rewards. Some hadiths state that reading Surat al-Ikhlas is equivalent to reading one third of the Qur'an. Speaking of this sura, the Prophet (pbuh) says, *"I swear to Allah that it is equal to reading one third of the Qur'an"* (Bukhari, Fada'il al-Qur'an, 13). One ear of corn grows from one kernel of corn; from that one ear of corn it is possible to produce a field of corn. In that field there may be hundreds of stalks, on each stalk there may be several ears; in short, from one kernel of corn, hundreds and thousands of kernels can be produced. In the same way, it could be said that every letter of the Surat al-Ikhlas will yield the same reward as if 1,500 letters were read.

Teaching the Qur'an is as great a virtue as learning it. Moreover, since teaching is the first step, teachers of the Qur'an share the rewards that are acquired by the learners. For this reason, the voices of teachers and students have filled mosques like bees buzzing in a hive since the time of the Prophet (pbuh). Some of the companions devoted their lives to teaching the Qur'an. Scholars who were solely devoted to teaching the Qur'an succeeded the companions of the Prophet (pbuh) in making a great effort to spread the Qur'an in every sphere of society; they turned mosques into schools. The Prophet (pbuh) says of the virtue of teaching the Qur'an, *"The most virtuous among you is he who teaches and learns the Qur'an"* (Bukhari, Fada'il al-Qur'an, 21). This hadith emphasizes the equal level of virtue of both those who teach and those who learn. Thus, one way to do good deeds, and to combine the two acts of learning and teaching is to understand the Qur'an and to recite it to others.

As much as learning the Qur'an is praised, so is forgetting it condemned. The people who have learned to read the Qur'an or have memorized a sura should be very careful, and repeat what they have learned continuously. Otherwise they can forget the sura they have memorized or how to read the Qur'an. Learning the Qur'an is a good deed; forgetting it is a bad one. Some scholars have claimed that if one fails to read the Qur'an for forty days then this is a sin. In a hadith it is stated that it is not appropriate to say that "I've forgotten that sura" even if some suras have been forgotten. It might imply that not reading the Qur'an means that you have abandoned it. In fact, it is the Qur'an that abandons people, not the other way round. The Prophet (pbuh) says, *"Why do the people say, 'I have forgotten such-and-such a sura (of the Qur'an)?' He, in fact, has been caused (by Allah) to forget"* (Bukhari, Fada'il al-Qur'an, 26). It can be understood from this hadith that saying "I have forgotten such-and-such a sura" is a sin. Thus, one commits a sin because they have abandoned the real Creator and have challenged Him.

Another interpretation is that what is condemned in this hadith is not the statement "I've forgotten" but the person's negligence that has lead to forgetting. To say "I've forgotten" instead of memorizing the sura is nothing more than negligence. The reply for abandoning the Qur'an on Doomsday is stated in the Qur'an:

"Then the Prophet will say: 'O my Lord! Truly My people took this Qur'an as a thing to be shunned'" (25:29-30).

It is necessary to read and repeat the Qur'an in order not to forget it. The same need is emphasized in a hadith with a wonderful analogy and it is stated that the Qur'an will escape the mind: *"Try to keep the Qur'an in your mind because it escapes people's minds faster than a camel released from its halter"* (Bukhari, Fada'il al-Qur'an, 23). Just like a camel cannot escape as long as it is tied up, the Qur'an will not be forgotten as long as it is recited.

Consigning the Qur'an to oblivion is not simply forgetting suras that have been memorized. When somebody stops reading the Qur'an for a while it is easily forgotten. For example, we take great pains to teach our children how to read the Qur'an during summer. When school opens and classes begin, reading the Qur'an stops and the three-month attempt is doomed to failure, necessitating us to start from the very beginning the next summer. All our efforts are wasted, and their reading skills have not improved. As children grow they tend to do other things in their summer vacations, and they do not listen to their parents, but rather act independently; it is in this way that children fail to learn the Qur'an despite their parents' wishes and efforts. To take the Qur'an out of the category of "holiday activities," children should be encouraged to read the Qur'an during the winter.

THE VIRTUES OF PARENTS' TEACHING THEIR CHILDREN HOW TO READ THE QUR'AN

We should have our children love the Qur'an before we start to teach it to them.

The Holy Qur'an should be taught to our children to stimulate and keep alive in them Islamic understanding. When teaching them how to read the Holy Qur'an, we should also stress its importance, and introduce its sacred contents. We should explain the role it played in the emergence of Islamic civilization in the past, and point out that it is the source of religious studies and morality. We should explain to them, in a suitable style, the role it played in the lives of Muslim scholars. We should remind them of the fact that scholars, such as Ibn Sina (Avicenna), who specialized in natural sciences and philosophy, and whose light blazed across many eras, not to mention many other scholars, started acquiring their knowledge by memorizing the Qur'an. We should have our children love the Qur'an before we start to teach it to them; we must use examples of how important the Qur'an is to the life of a Muslim.

Qur'anic education starts with teaching how to read it. But before this, children should love the Qur'an, and the foundation of this love should be laid by the family. Children who see their parents reading the Qur'an want to learn to read it too.

Due to the importance of the family in Qur'anic education, the Prophet (pbuh) described the rewards that parents would receive in the hereafter and mentioned the drawbacks of taking children along this path through fear of their worldly future. Under the influence of their innate sense of compassion, parents do not want their children to suffer, and they bring up their children with the same ideas. In order to correct this way of thinking, the Prophet (pbuh) reminds us of the divine rewards the teaching of the Qur'an will bring to parents. In one of his hadiths the Prophet (pbuh) says, *"All the sins - whether they be of the past or future - of the person who teaches his son how to read the Qur'an will be pardoned. Whoever teaches his son to recite the Qur'an will be raised up by Allah on the Day of Judgment shining like the full moon. His son will be asked to 'read.' For every verse the child reads, Allah will raise the level of the father until the child reaches the final verse that he can recite"* (Majma' al-Zawa'id, 7, 165,166). Although fathers and sons are mentioned in the hadith, the reference is to both mother and father, and sons and daughters. Mentioning the specific while referring to the general is a characteristic of the Qur'an and sunna.

By not making worldly interests their goal, parents will gain incalculable merits and rewards if they encourage their children to learn to read the Qur'an. In a hadith, which tells how the Qur'an will intercede in the hereafter, the Prophet (pbuh) describes the situation as follows: *"The parents of those who read the Qur'an will be clad with two outfits whose value cannot be apprised in worldly terms. They will ask, 'Why have we been given this clothing?' They will be told, 'because your child read the Qur'an and practiced it"* (Darimi, Fada'il al-Qur'an, 15). This hadith emphasizes not only the virtue of knowing how to read the Qur'an, but also the virtue of loving it and of arranging one's life according to Qur'anic principles. In order to practice the Qur'an, Qur'anic education should not be limited to reading and memorization. Practicing the Qur'an can only be realized if a continuous and permanent relationship with it has been established, if the curiosity in our children is stimulated, and if its contents are taught. Children should first be read the parables of the Prophets in the Qur'an, from translations or commentaries on the Qur'an. They should be encouraged to love the Qur'an by emphasizing examples that they can comprehend. Since the minds of children are predisposed to comprehending stories and examples, these parables will have a permanent impact on their minds and shape the worlds of their imagination. They will learn the concepts of good and evil from these parables, and thus the light of the Qur'an will be the primary force that shapes their thinking. Moreover, they should be taught translations of the short suras. They should be taught the meaning of the texts they have memorized and rote memorization should be avoided.

The Prophet (pbuh) tells of the rewards that the parents of the servants of the Qur'an will achieve: "*The parents of whoever reads the Qur'an and acts upon what is in it will be crowned on the day of Judgment, the light of which will be greater than the light of the sun if it were to be contained in a worldly house, therefore, what do you think the reward of the person would be who (actually) acts upon it?*" (meaning the reward of the child) (Abu Dawud, Witr, 14). This hadith speaks of the merits that will be gained by the parents of those who accept the principles of the Qur'an and who apply them to their lives. However, this hadith does not describe the merits they will gain, and implies that their rewards cannot be likened to anything in this world.

Reading and practicing the Qur'an will enable not only the parents to be saved, but also other members of the family. The Qur'an will intercede alongside the Prophet (pbuh). The Qur'an will not only intercede for those servants who have applied Qur'anic principles to their lives and who teach such principles to others, but it will also intercede for the members of the family. This is seen in the following hadith: "*Allah puts in paradise he who reads and practices the Qur'an. The Qur'an will intercede for ten members of his family who are destined for Hell*" (Ibn Maja, 16).

THE VIRTUES OF READING THE QUR'AN

"Whoever reads one hundred verses a night will not be written down as negligent."

Of all creatures, only human beings have the ability to speak and read. The Prophet (pbuh) is ordered to "read" in the first revelations: *"Read! In the Name of your Lord, Who created: He created man from a clot. Read, by your All-Generous Lord..."* (96:1-3). Reading is the first step to obtaining information and knowledge. Since it is the main source that includes fundamental information concerning knowledge, morality, education, and behavior, the Qur'an deserves to be read more than any other literature. Thus, not only did the Prophet (pbuh) spend much time reading the Qur'an, he also encouraged his followers to read it in many of his hadiths. He likened those who read the Qur'an to fruit: *"The example of a believer who recites the Qur'an is that of a citron (a type of citrus fruit) which is good in taste and aroma. And the believer who does not recite the Qur'an is like a date which has a good taste but no aroma. And the example of an impious person who recites the Qur'an is that of Rihana (an aromatic plant) which smells good but is bitter in taste. And the example of an impious person who does not recite the Qur'an is that of a colocynth which is bitter in taste and has no aroma"* (Bukhari, Fada'il al-Qur'an, 17). Both the taste and the aroma of the believer who reads the Qur'an are good. He has learned the truths in the Qur'an and has tasted the spiritual pleasures in reading it. The Qur'an finds its true meaning in the soul, heart, and mouth of the believer. In this way his good behavior diffuses fragrance to his surroundings; those around become elated. The believer who does not read the Qur'an cannot influence others, despite having tasted faith and achieved the sweetness of the Qur'an. Those around him cannot make use of his fragrance. The hadith likens the believers who read the Qur'an to a citrus fruit. The inside of the fruit is sweet; and it smells good when it is peeled. Faith makes the interior beautiful, while reading the Qur'an reflects the beauty inside and enables the unity of the interior and the exterior.

Those who learn the Qur'an will inevitably encounter some difficulties in the beginning and make mistakes. Some might think reading the Qur'an in this way is disrespectful. To prevent such a fear, the Prophet (pbuh) says, *"He who recites the Qur'an is with honorable angels. He who reads the Qur'an even though they encounter difficulties gains two merits"* (Bukhari, Tafsir, 80). A similar hadith says, *"A person who is skilled in reading the Qur'an is accompanied by munificent and obedient angels called 'safarah'. For he who reads the Qur'an, although he can hardly read it, the merit is twice"* (Abu Dawud, Witr, 14). The first merit is the reward for reading the Qur'an; the second is for reading it with difficulty. In these hadiths it is indicated that attempts to read the Qur'an and listen to subjects related to it, despite hardship and difficulty are esteemed by Allah.

People want to imitate others and have the worldly possessions that others own. Sometimes they want to be the sole owners of these possessions; this is jealousy. Sometimes they want to acquire the beauties others have; this is envy. Islam forbids jealousy. But it is not wrong to envy the virtue of others. Unfortunately, people mostly envy the wrong things and they long for riches and property. In fact, there are two types of people that should be envied. The Prophet (pbuh) describes these two types of people who are worth envying as follows:

"Do not wish to be like anybody except in two cases: A man to whom Allah has taught the Qur'an and whom recites it during the hours of the night and during the hours of the day, and his neighbor listens to him and says, 'I wish I had been given what has been given to so-and-so, so that I

might do what he does'; and a man to whom Allah has given wealth and who spends it on what is just and right, whereupon another man may say, 'I wish I had been given what so-and-so has been given, for then I would do what he does'" (Bukhari, Fada'il al-Qur'an, 20).

This hadith says that there is no one else worth envying. Some people do not have the means to give alms. These people can gain the merits that the rich gain by spending their riches. The hadith gives the model person for all spheres of society, be they rich or poor.

Reading the Qur'an is one of the most virtuous prayers. Supererogatory prayers, dhikr (remembrance of Allah), or prayers performed to meet some urgent need should not prevent us from reading the Qur'an. More than unique merits and virtues, reading the Qur'an also grants us the acquisition of the rewards that can be gained by other virtuous activities. So those who read the Qur'an should not worry when they cannot pray or when they neglect some virtuous dhikr. Reading the Qur'an is a form of prayer, too. The Prophet (pbuh) describes the situation in one of his hadiths: "*Allah has ordered: 'If ever reading the Qur'an and reciting My names prevents anyone from asking for what he needs from Me, I'll give him more than I grant those who want them'*" (Darimi, Fada'il al-Qur'an, 20).

It is also virtuous to listen to the Qur'an. A hadith says, "*Those who listen to a verse from the Qur'an will be granted sawabs many times over. For he who is reciting, the verse becomes a light on Doomsday*" (Ahmad ibn Hanbal, 2, 341). It has been related that angels come to listen when the Qur'an is read at night, and that some of the companions witnessed this during the time of the Prophet (pbuh), (Bukhari, Fada'il al-Qur'an, 15). The Prophet (pbuh) had some of his companions read the Qur'an, and listened to it because of the virtue of listening to it. When some hesitated, saying, "*O Allah's Prophet, Shall I recite (the Qur'an) to you when it has been revealed to you?*" the Prophet (pbuh) replied, '*I like hearing it from another person*'" (Bukhari, Fada'il al-Qur'an, 32-35).

The Qur'an should be read day and night, with no special time being designated for it. A hadith says, "*The person who reads the Qur'an openly is like the person who gives alms openly. The person who reads the Qur'an secretly is like the person who gives alms secretly*" (Tirmidhi, Sawab al-Qur'an, 20). Just like giving alms openly encourages others to do the same, so does reading the Qur'an openly. To be alone with the Qur'an in the darkness of night is like giving alms secretly. In privacy, a person will search for a place in the Qur'an, because it is important for every believer to seek a place in the Qur'an and to act in accordance with this place.

The Qur'an is not only a book from which religious rules are derived; it is also a book of wisdom, contemplation, obedience, communication, invitation, dhikr, and prayers. These are all matters that need regular repetition. For this reason, the Qur'an should be read frequently. Although there are different views over the frequency of reading, the hadith advises that the entire Qur'an be read once a month. The Prophet (pbuh) says in a hadith, *"Whoever reads one hundred verses a night will not be written down as negligent"* and in another, *"Whoever reads one hundred verses a night will be granted sawabs for a full night's prayer"* (Darimi, Fada'il al-Qur'an, 28). It is apparent in this hadith how virtuous it is to read the Qur'an. The number of verses given is not in order to set a certain limit, but rather to encourage reading the Qur'an; in other hadiths other quantities are mentioned. If one wants to plan certain periods for reading the Qur'an according to the Prophet's orders and advice, it is sunna to make a habit of reading the Qur'an from beginning to end once a month; this has been arrived at by taking into account the Prophet's advice to his companions (Abu Dawud, Salat, 325).

The reading of the Qur'an should be done with gravity. One should read it in one's best voice and manner. Allah commanded the Prophet (pbuh) to "serve the Lord" and "rehearse the Qur'an" (27:91-92) and advised him to "recite the Qur'an in slow, measured, rhythmic tones" (73:4). The Prophet (pbuh) ordered that the Qur'an should be recited beautifully, and he chose those of his companions who could recite well to do so, and he listened to them. Having asked 'Abd Allah ibn Mas'ud to recite the Qur'an for him, the Prophet (pbuh) shed tears after the verses were read, (Fada'il al-Qur'an). The Prophet (pbuh) advised that it should be recited in a mournful mood, saying that it was revealed in sorrow. He praised recitals of the Qur'an that increased feelings of fear and respect toward Allah (Majma' al-Zawa'id, 7,170).

The Prophet (pbuh) loved reading the Qur'an to such a degree that when he had finished reading it, he would turn to the beginning and start again. He said that it was "the most virtuous of good deeds" to read the Qur'an without taking a break. Comparing this to being a nomad, the Prophet (pbuh) said, *"The friend of the Qur'an goes from its beginning to its end and from its end to its beginning; whenever he stops (having read it all) he moves on (and starts anew)"* (Darimi, Fada'il al-Qur'an, 33). When the Qur'an has been recited from the beginning to the end, it is as if the journey in the universe of the Qur'an ended; when reading starts anew with the surat al-Fatiha, it is a new journey being embarked on in the same universe.

The Prophet (pbuh) described such a situation using the words "stop" and "move on." This is the reason why some people who finish reading the Book from the beginning to the end read surat al-Fatiha and the first five verses of surat al-Baqara before putting it to one side. In this way, the Qur'an has not been laid aside with the intention of taking a break after having read it, but rather the person reading has made the reading of it a habit.

There are many virtues inherent in reading the complete Qur'an. From the moment the Qur'an was revealed, people started to memorize it. As a result of this practice, which was adopted as a tradition in Islamic society, the Qur'an spread to every sphere of society. Besides memorizing the Qur'an, reading it from the beginning to end is a virtuous act. The Prophet (pbuh) said, *"Whoever performs his prayer will have a petition accepted. Whoever reads the Qur'an from beginning to end also has a petition accepted"* (Majma' al-Zawa'id, 7, 172). On hearing this hadith, Anas ibn Malik, one of the companions, would summon his family and pray for them after having completed reading the Qur'an from beginning to end.

When the Qur'an is read sincerely and genuinely it revitalizes one's soul, heart, and emotions. Listening to its recitation as if one were listening to the speech of the Prophet (pbuh) gives one eternal bliss. Moving one step higher and listening to it as if Archangel Gabriel speaks directly to him earns one's soul indescribable contentment. Listening to it as if one is the direct addressee of Allah, elevates that person to the empyrean world. It is in search of this that people spent their lives in the past and still spend their lives now reciting the Qur'an. They derive inexpressible pleasures from reading it.

THE REWARDS FOR READING THE QUR'AN

"One who recites the first three verses of
Surat al-Kahf is safe from Satan's mischief."

To be able to read the Qur'an is the greatest reward in this world. That the Qur'an will come in front of people in some unfathomable nature is related in several hadiths. It is possible that the Qur'an itself will confront people in some way. Some scholars have argued that such statements suggest the personification of rewards for reading the Qur'an. Many hadiths relate that the Qur'an will intercede for people on Doomsday. One of them tells about the personification of the Qur'an and its suras on Doomsday as follows: *"There comes the Qur'an and those who practiced it in the world. The suras al-Baqara and Al-i 'Imran come at the beginning of the Qur'an. Those two suras come like two awnings from the intersection of which light floods through, or like a flock of birds with their wings open, and they fight for the salvation of those who read and practiced the Qur'an"* (Tirmidhi, Fada'il al-Qur'an, 4). Thus we must respect the Qur'an. We should not neglect reading it by saying that we already pray; we should in no way offend it.

The reading of it purifies people's souls, it cures them, and saves them from both physical and spiritual ailments. A hadith says, *"One who recites the first three verses of the Surat al-Kahf is safe from Satan's mischief"* (Tirmidhi, Fada'il al-Qur'an, 5). This hadith informs us that it is possible to distance ourselves from the evil that affects our souls and minds, evil such as the mischief of Satan, by reciting the Surat al-Kahf.

Reading the Qur'an is not only a prayer that has divine results. It is also recommended that the Qur'an be recited in order to distance ourselves from the evil that might confront people at night. People may feel uneasiness when they go to bed, due to physical or spiritual causes. One should trust in Allah and take shelter in the protection of the Qur'an in order to assure the heart's safety and to attain inner peace. A hadith says, *"If somebody recites the last two verses of Surat al-Baqara at night, that will be suffi-*

cient for him" (Bukhari, Fada'il al-Qur'an, 27). Some other hadiths inform us that those who recite Ayat al-Kursi when they go to bed will be protected by one of Allah's angels and the devil will not be able to get near him, (Bukhari, Fada'il al-Qur'an, 10).

The verses of the Qur'an do not simply comprise sentences that convey ideas. Because the Qur'an is the word of Allah, it has a miraculous power that exceeds contemplation. This is described as follows in one of the verses:

"And We reveal of the Qur'an that which is healing and merciful for the believers, and it yields nothing but perdition to the wrongdoers" (17:82).

As mentioned in the verse, the Qur'an is a source of remedy for our physical and spiritual ailments. The Prophet (pbuh) recommends that al-Fatiha be recited for the ill; he recited al-Falaq and an-Nas when he was ill, (Bukhari, Fada'il al-Qur'an, 9). Moreover, Aisha, the mother of Muslims, relates that the Prophet (pbuh) would recite the suras of al-Ikhlas, al-Falaq, and an-Nas every night when he went to bed and would blow into his hands and rub his hands over his body (Bukhari, Fada'il al-Qur'an, 14).

As can be seen in the hadiths, the Prophet (pbuh) left behind for us the Qur'an as a most valuable inheritance. He orders that we adhere to it when dissension becomes widespread, when turmoil in society intensifies, and when disorder reigns. It is our responsibility as his followers to observe his advice and orders. If we do not want to become a derelict house ourselves and to turn our houses into our graves, then we should adorn our homes with the recitation of the Qur'an, we should whisper it into the ears of our babies, and pour its love into the hearts of our children so that 'Islam will be the most stentorian voice in the future.' It would be appropriate to end this discussion with a prayer:

"O the light that descended in Makka and ascended in Madina. It is not like you to hide; remove the veil from your radiant face so that eyes steeped in vices can see the beauty in you, so that we can be drawn to your light anew."